Johann Reinhold Forster

A Catalogue of the Animals of North America

Johann Reinhold Forster

A Catalogue of the Animals of North America

ISBN/EAN: 9783741184390

Manufactured in Europe, USA, Canada, Australia, Japa

Cover: Foto ©Andreas Hilbeck / pixelio.de

Manufactured and distributed by brebook publishing software
(www.brebook.com)

Johann Reinhold Forster

A Catalogue of the Animals of North America

Little Falcon.
Falco Sparverius, LINN.

M. Griffith Pinx.ᵗ   R. Murray Sc.ᵗ

A
CATALOGUE
OF THE
ANIMALS
OF
NORTH AMERICA.

CONTAINING,

An Enumeration of the known QUADRUPEDS, BIRDS, REPTILES, FISH, INSECTS, Cruftaceous and Teftaceous ANIMALS; many of which are New, and never defcribed before.

To which are added,

SHORT DIRECTIONS
FOR

COLLECTING, PRESERVING, and TRANSPORTING, all Kinds of

NATURAL HISTORY CURIOSITIES.

By JOHN REINHOLD FORSTER, F A.S.

Non ad unam Natura formam opus fuum præftat; fed in ipfa varietate fe jactat.
SENECA, Quæft. Nat. VII. 27.

LONDON:
Sold by B. WHITE, at Horace's Head, in Fleet-Street.

M.DCC.LXXI.

T O

MARMADUKE TUNSTALL, Esq.

Dear S I R,

THE repeated favours *You* were fo kind to beſtow upon me, in the compaſs of a ſhort acquaintance, and the zeal with which *You* promote the great cauſe of Natural Hiſtory ; encouraged me to prefix *Your* Name to this Publication, and give me an opportunity, thus publicly, to acknowledge the aſſiſtance *Your* benevolent and generous friend-ſhip favoured me with.

Nothing is left to me, but the ſimple mention of thanks ; and my ſincere wiſhes for *Your* health, happineſs, and the enjoyment of every intellectual and moral bleſſing. I am, with the trueſt regard,

Dear S I R,

your moſt obliged,

obedient,

humble Servant,

JOHN REINHOLD FORSTER

London, April 24, 1771.

To the READER.

I Had hinted in the Preface to the third volume of *Kalm's* Travels, that I could publish but an imperfect and small catalogue of *North American* animals; and therefore declined to give it. Since that time, I have been pressed by some worthy friends to publish that catalogue, such as it is; and what is still more, I have been favoured with ample materials by a Gentleman, who is forming a collection for a Natural History of *North America*, and hopes by this to incite the inquisitive and learned resident in that country, to search, and to transmit to their friends in *England*, the productions of their several provinces. The Zoology of the first four classes of animals in *Great Britain*, has been very accurately and compleatly published; that of the country of the descendants of *Great-Britain* ought with most propriety to follow, as it interests the Mother Country most. These reasons had a great weight with me; and I offer this small catalogue merely as an essay towards forming a more compleat Natural History of that extensive continent. To instruct the Collectors, I have added to this list some short directions for the best method of preserving and transporting the various subjects of Natural History.

The Quadrupeds of this list are referred to the Synopsis of Quadrupeds of Mr. *Pennant*; the Birds, Fish, Reptiles, Insects, and *Crustacea*, to *Linnæus*, *Brisson*, Mr. *Edwards*,

and

and *Catesby*; some few excepted, which are referred to the *Planches enluminées*, published at *Paris*, and marked here *Pl. enl.* so as *Catesby* with a single *C.* and those which are common to *Great Britain* and *America*, to the *British* Zoology.

The Animals which have recently been discovered in *North America*, or overlooked by Mr. *Catesby*, are distinguished by *N. S.* marking a *New Species*; and by *B.* and *Muf. Bl.* The first authority is from a Collection formed by a Gentleman in his voyage to *Newfoundland*; the second, from a most select and numerous Collection of *American* Animals, belonging to a Lady in *Lancashire*.

The New Species, in the Catalogue of Birds, I had leave to insert here from Mr. *Pennant*'s manuscript; and those of Insects are taken from my own manuscript descriptions of such Insects as were not described by Dr. *Linnæus*.

The print prefixed here represents an elegant little Falcon, drawn and engraved from a fine specimen lately brought over from *North America*.

N. B. *The Animals marked* E *are of* European *Origin; having been introduced there by the* Spaniards *or* English, *after the discovery of the New World: and those marked* Eur. *are originally natives of both Continents.*

CLASS I. QUADRUPEDS.

DIV. I. HOOFED.

SECT. I. WHOLE HOOFED.

Genus.			syn. quad.
I. HORSE	Generous	E.	Nº 1
	Afs	E.	3

SECT. II. CLOVEN HOOFED.

II. SHEEP	Common	E.	8
III. GOAT	Domeſtic	E.	p. 14
IV. DEER	Elk, or Moofe,	Eur.	Nº 35
	Rein	Eur.	36
	Stag	Eur.	38
	Virginian	N. S.	39
	Roe?		43
V. HOG	Common	E.	54

DIV. II. DIGITATED QUADRUPEDS.

VI. DOG	Faithful	E.	Nº 110
	Wolf	Eur.	111
	Fox	Eur.	112
	Arctic	Eur.	113
	Grey		114
	Silvery		115
VII. CAT	Brown		129
	Common	E.	133
	Lynx	Eur.	135
	Bay Lynx	N. S.	136

VIII.

A 4   Field

CLASS II. BIRDS.

DIV. I. LAND BIRDS.

SECT. I. RAPACIOUS.

I. VULTURE.	Carrion. V. aura. 122. C. I. 6.
II. FALCON	Bald Eagle	F. leucocephalus. C. I. 1.
	Sea	F. offifragus. in exhibitions
	Ringtail	F. Fulvus. *Edw.* I.
	Black-bellied	N. S.
	White	*Du Pratz*, II. 75.
	Oſprey	F. Haliaëtus. C. I. 2.

Gentil

	Gentil Falcon	F. gentilis *Mr. B*
	Goshawk	F. palumbarius. *Lawson*
	Ashcoloured	*Edw.* 53.
	Sacre	*Mr. B. de Buffon*
	Winter	N. S. *Muf. Bl.*
	Dusky	*Edw.* 3. 4.
	Rough-footed	N. S. *Mr. B.*
	Chocolate	N. S. *do.*
	Marsh	*Edw.* 291.
	Buzzard	F. Buteo. *Mr. B.*
	White-rump'd	F. Hudsonius. *Edw.* 107.
	Fork-tail	F. furcatus. C. I. 4.
	Pigeon	F. columbarius. C. I. 3.
	Little	F. sparverius. C. I. 5.

*

III. OWL

	Great	Strix bubo. *Edw.* 60
	Short-eared	*Br. Zool. Muf. Bl.*
	Red	St. Asio C. I. 7.
	Mottled	N. S. *Muf. Bl.*

* *

	Snowy	St. nyctea. *Edw.* 61
	Barred	N. S. *Muf. Bl.*
	Canada	*Br.* I. 518.
	Brown	*Br. Zool. Mr. B.*
	White	*ib.*
	Hawk	*Edw.* 62.
	Little.	*Muf. Bl. Br. Zool.*

IV. SHRIKE

	Cinereous.	Lanius excubitor. C. *app.*
	Crested.	L. Canadensis
	Louisiane.	*Pl. enl.* 397.

SECT. II. PIES.

V. PARROT

	Caroline.	Psittacus Carolinensis. C. I. 11.
	Illinois.	Ps. pertinax. *Edw.* 234. *Br.*

VI. CROW

	Raven.	*Br. Zool. Mr. B.*
	Carrion.	*B. Zool. Muf. Bl.*
	Magpie	*Br. Zool. Edw.* p. 126.
	Cinereous	C. Canadensis
	Blue.	C. cristatus. C. I. 15.

VII.

VII. ORIOLE	Redwing	Oriolus Phœniceus.	C. I.	13
	Baltimore	O. Baltimorus		48
	Spurious	O. Spurius		49
	Brown-headed	N. S. *Mr Kuckahn*		

| VIII. GRACULE | Shining | Gracula quiscula | C. I. | 12 |

| IX. CUCKOO | Caroline | Cuculus Americanus. | C. I. | 9. |

X. WOODPECKER	White-billed.	Picus principalis	C. I.	16
	Buff-cheeked	P. pileatus	C. I.	17
	Gold-wing	P. auratus		18
	Scarlet	P. erythrocephalus		20
	Red-bellied	P. Carolinus		19
	Spotted	*Br. Zool.* I. 178. *Muf. Bl.*		
	Hairy.	P. villofus		19
	Yellow-bellied	P. varius		21
	Little	P. pubefcens		*ib.*
	Black	*Albin*		
	Three-toed	P. tridactylus. *Edw.*		

XI. NUTHATCH.	Greater	*Br. Zool.*		22
	Leffer			*ib.*
	Canada	*Br.* III. 593		

| XII. KINGFISHER | Great | Alcedo alcyon | | 69 |
| | Louifiane. | *Pratz.* II. 82 | | |

| XIII. CREEPER | Bahama | Certhia flaveola | | 59 |
| | Common | *Br. Zool. Muf. Bl.* | | |

| XIV. HUMMER | Red-throated | Trochilus colubris | C. I. | 65 |

SECT. III. GALLINACEOUS.

XV. TURKY	Wild	Meleagris Gallopavo.		
	†			
XVI. GROUS	Ruffed	Tetrao umbellus	*Edw.*	248
	Pinnated	T. cupido	C. III.	1.
	Long-tailed	T. Phafianellus	*Edw.*	117
	Spotted	T. Canadenfis	*Edw.* 71, III.
	White	T. Lagopus	*Edw.*	72
	† †			
	Partridge	T. Virginianus	C. III.	12
	Quail ?	T. Mexicanus		

SECT.

SECT. IV. COLUMBINE.

SECT. V. PASSERINE.

Painted   E. Ciris C. 44 *Edw.* 130. 273
Louifiane   E. Ludoviciana.
Blue ?   *Br.* III.   298

XXIII. TANAGRE Blue   Tanagra cyanea   C. I. 45
          Green   ·Motacilla guira *Edw.* 351. *Muf Bl.*
          Bifhop   T. Epifcopus. Du Pratz. II. 94
          Red   T. rubra   C. I. 56

XXIV. FINCH Towhe   Fringilla Erythrophthalma 34
          Golden   Fr. triftis   43
          Orange   Fr. zena   42
          Mountain Fr. montana   *Edw.* 269
          Little   C. I. 35
          Cow pen   34
          Bahama   Fr. bicolor. 37
          Caroline *Pl. en.* 181. 223 ?
          White-throated *Edw.* 304
          Ferruginous *Edw.* 354. *Pr.* III. 296
          Crimfon head N. S. *Muf. Bl.*
          Fafciated   N. S. *Do.*
          Greater red-poll. *Br. Zool. Muf. Bl.*

XXV. FLY-CATCHER Tyrant   Lanius tyrannus   C. I. 55
                 Fork tail Mufcicapa tyrannua
                 Chattering C. I. 50
                 Crefted   Mufc. crinita C. I. 52
                 Black-cap C. I. 53
                 Cinereous Mufc. virens
                 Red-eyed M. olivacea C. I. 54
                 Cat   M. Carolinenfis 66
                 Canada   M. Canadenfis
                 Blue   Motacilla fialis C. I. 47
                 Brown   C. I. 54

XXVI. LARK Shore   Alauda alpeftris C. I. 32
          Red   *Br. Zool Edw.* 197
          Calandre *Edw.* 268

XXVII. WAGTAIL Redftart Mufcicapa ruticilla. C. I. 67
              Yellow breaft Turdus trichas. *Edw.* 237
              Black throat Motacilla Canadenfis. *Edw.* 252
              Yellow throat. C. I. 62.
              Yellow rump. *Edw.* 255

                                             Red

Red poll	M. petechia.	*Edw.* 256
Black poll		
Pine	Certhia pinus.	C. I. 61.
Crowned	M. coronata.	*Edw.* 298
Golden wing	M. chryfoptera.	*Edw.* 299
Green	*Edw.* 300	
Pied	*Edw. ib.* M. varia	
Bloodyfide	M. Penfylvanica.	*Edw.* 301
Cœrulean	M. cœrulea.	*Edw.* 302
Worm-eater.	*Edw.* 305	
Yellow	*Br.* III. 492	
Louifiane		500
Great		508
Quebec	M. Icterocephala	
Yellow-tailed ?	*Edw.* 257	
Spotted	*Edw.* 257	
Cinereous	*Br.* III. 524	
Olive	*Pl. enl.* 58	
Ruby-crowned	M. calendula.	*Edw.* 254
Golden-crefted.	*Br. Zool. C. App.*	
Yellow	*Br. Zool.* II. 266.	*Edw.*
Wren	*Muf. Bl.*	

XXVIII. Titmouse

Crefted	Parus bicolor. C. I. 57
Hooded	C. I. 60
Virginian	P. Virginianus. C. I. 58
American	P. Americanus 64
Canada	*Br.* III. 553.
Colemoufe	*Br. Zool. Mr. B.*

XXIX. Swallow

Houfe	*Br. Zool. Mr. B.*
Martin	*ib. Muf. Bl.*
Sand	*ib. C. App.*
Swift	*ib. Lawfon*
Purple	Hirundo purpurea. C. I. 51
Canada	H. fubis. *Edw.* 120
Aculeated	H. pelafgia. C. III. 8

XXX. Goatsucker.

Common	*Br. Zool.* C. I. 8
Leffer	Capr. minor. C. III. 16.

DIV. II. WATER FOWL.

SECT. VI. CLOVEN-FOOTED.

*

XXX I. HERON.	Hooping	Ardea Americanus. C. I. 75
	Canada	A. Canadenfis. *Edw.* 133
	Brown	A. Herodias. *Edw.* 136

* *

	Common	*Br. Zool.* C. *App.*
	Violet	A. violacea. C. I. 79
	Blue	A. cœrulea 76
	Cinereous	*Edw.* 135
	Great white	A. alba. *Muf. Bl.*
	Little white	A. æquinoctialis. C. I. 77
	Green	A. virens. 80
	Bittern	A. Hudfonias. *Edw.* 135
	Minute	*Br. Zool. Muf. Bl.*
	Caroline	C. I. 78
	Green head	*Mr. Kuckahn*

XXXII. IBIS	Wood	Tantalus loculator. C. I. 81
	Scarlet	T. ruber 84
	White	T. albus 82
	Brown	T. fufcus 83

| XXXIII. CURLEW | Efkimaux | N. S. *Mr. B.* |

XXXIV. WOODCOCK.	American	*Muf. Bl.*
	Snipe	*Br. Zool. Muf. Bl.*
	Jack	*ib. Muf. Bl.*
	Godwit	*ib. C. App.*
	Red	*ib. Edw.* 138
	Great	Scolopax fedoa. *Edw.* 137
	Nodding	N. S. *Mr. B.*
	Spotted	*Muf. Bl.*

XXXV. SAND-PIPER	Turnftone	Tringa interpres *Edw.* 141
	Common	*Br. Zool. Mr. Kuckahn*
	Spotted	*ib. Edw.* 270
	Cinereous	*ib. Mr. B.*

Knot

	Knot	*ib. Edw.* 276
	Redſhank	*ib. C. App.*
	Grey Pl.	*ib. C. App.*
	Purre	*ib. Muſ. Dl.*
	Little	N. S.
	Gloſſey	*Mr. B.* N. S.
	Green	*Br. Zool. Mr. Kuckahn*
XXXVI. PLOVER	Green	*Br. Zool. Muſ. Bl.*
	Pie	*ib.* C. I. 85
	Noiſy	Charadrius vociferus. C. 1. 71
	Golden	Ch. apricarius *Edw.* 140
	Lark	*Br. Zool. Muſ. Bl.*
	Sanderling	*ib. Muſ. Bl.*
XXXVII. RAIL	Clapper	*Muſ. Bl.*
	Red-breaſted	*Edw.* 279
XXXVIII. WATER-HEN	Caroline	Rallus Carolinus. *Edw.* 144. C. I. 70.
	Common	*Br. Zool. Muſ. Bl.*

SECT. VII. With PINNATED FEET.

XXXIX. COOT	Common	*Br. Zool. Muſ. Bl.*
XL. PHALAROPE	Grey	*ib. Edw.* 308
	Red.	*Edw.* 142
	Brown	*Edw.* 46
XLI. GREBE,	Eared	*Edw.* 96
	Pied bill	C. I. 91.

SECT. VIII. WEBBED-FOOTED.

XLII. FLAMMANT	Red	Phænicopterus ruber. C. I. 73
XLIII. AUK	Great	*Br. Zool. Edw.* 147
	Razor	*ib. Edw.* 358
	Puffin	*ib. Edw. ib.*
	New	N. S. *Br. Muſ.*
	Little	*Br. Zool. Edw.* 91
	Guillemot	*ib. Edw.* 359
	Black	*ib.*

XLIV.

XLIV. Diver	Northern	*Br. Zool. Muf. Bl.*
	Immer	Colymbus Immer. *Muf. Bl.*
	Speckled	*Br. Zool. Muf. Bl.*
	Lumme	*ib. Edw.* 97. 146
XLV. Cut-water	Black	Rhynchops nigra. C. I. 9⊕
XLVI. Tern	Noddy	Sterna ftolida. C. I. 88
	Black	*Br. Zool. Kalm*
	Greater	*ib. Muf. Bl.*
	Leffer	*ib. Muf. Bl.*
XLVII. Gull	Great	*ib. Mr. B.*
	Wagel	*ib.*
	Herring	*ib.*
	Kittiwake	*ib.*
	Laughing	*ib.*
	Black toed	*ib.*
	Arctic	*ib. Edw.* 148, 149.
XLVIII. Petrel	Fulmar	*ib.*
	Shear water	*ib. Edw.* 359
	Storm	*ib. Edw.* 91
XLIX. Saw-bill.	Goofander	*Br. Zool. Muf. Bl.*
	Redbreafted	*ib. Edw.* 95.
	Hooded	Mergus cucullatus. *Edw.* 360
	Smew	*Br. Zool. Muf. Bl.*
L. Duck	Swan	*ib. Edw.* 150
	Canada	Anas Canadenfis. *Edw.* 151
	Wild-goofe	*Br. Zool.*
	White-fronted	*ib. Edw.* 153
	Blue	A. cærulefcens. *Edw.* 152
	Bernacle	*Br. Zool.*
	Brant	*ib.*
	Snow	Anfer niveus. *Br.* VI. *Lawfon*
	Eider	*Br. Zool Edw.* 98
	King	A. fpectabilis. *Edw.* 154
	Velvet	*Br. Zool. Muf. Bl.*
	Black	A. perfpicillata. *Edw.* 155
	Shoveler	*Br. Zool.* C. I. 96. *fœm.*
	Golden eye	*ib. Muf. Bl.*
	Harlequin	A. hiftrionica. C. I. 98. *fœm.*
		[*Edw.* 99. 157.

Pied

	Pied	A. albeola. *Edw.* 100
	Pochard	*Br. Zool. C. App.*
	Pin-tail	*ib. Muf. Bl.*
	Swallow-tail	*ib. Edw.* 280
	Buffel	A. Bucephala. C. I. 95
	White-faced	A. difcors. C. I. 100
	Ilathera	A. Bahamenfis. C. I. 93
	Brown	*Mr. B.*
	Summer	A. fponfa. *Edw.* 101. C. I. 97.
	Widgeon	*Br. Zool. Muf. Bl.*
	Teal	*ib. Mr. B.*
	Blue-wing	C. I. 99.
	Mallard	*Br. Zool. C. App.*
	Scaup	*ib. Muf. Bl.*
LI. Pelecan	Pelecan	*Edw.* 93.
	Corvorant	*Br. Zool. Muf. Bl.*
	Shag	*ib. C. App.*
	Gannet	*Mr. B. Br. Zool.*

CLASS III. REPTILES.

SECT. I. With Four Feet.

I. Tortoise	Green	Teftudo Mydas C. II.	38
	Hawkfbill	T. caretta	39
	Logger-head		40
	Trunk		
	Chequered	T. Carolina.	*Edw.* 205
	Mud		*Edw.* 287
	Rough ?	T. fcabra	
	Indented ?	T. denticulata	
	River	N. S. *Dr. Garden*	
II. Frog	Bull	Rana ocellata.	C. II. 72
	Land		C. 69
	Water		C. 70
		B	Green

	Green		C. 71
	Horned	R. cornuta	
	Striped	N. S. Mr. *Ellis*	
III. Lizard	Allegator	Lacerta Crocodylus.	C. II. 63
	Lion	L. fex-lineata	68
	Guano	L. Iguana	64
	Green		65
	Blue-tail	L. fafciata	67
	Spotted	L. punctata	III. 10
	Canada	N. S. Mr. *Ellis*	
	Annulated	*Muf. Bl.*	

SECT. II. With Two Feet.

| IV. Siren | Caroline | Siren Lacertina. *Ph. Tr.* LVI. 189 |

SECT. III. Without Feet.

V. Snake	† Rattle	Crotalus horridus	C. II. 41
	Leffer	Cr. miliarius	C. 4
	Chequered	Cr. Duriffus	
	† † Hog-nofe	Boa contortrix	C. 56
	† † † Striped	Coluber leberis	
	Wampum	Coluber fafciatus	C. 58
	Green	C. ordinatus	53
	Chain	C. getulus	52
	Ribbon	C. faurita	50
	Black	C. conftrictor	48
	Bead	C. guttatus	60
	Familiar	C. æftivus	57
	Porraceous	C. mycterizans	47
	Croffed	Coluber fimus	
	Smooth-headed	ftriatulus	
	Dotted	punctatus	
	Ringed	doliatus	
	Brown	fipedon	
	Yellow	fulvius	
	Vittated	firtalis	
			Water

CLASS IV. FISH.

SECT. I. CETACEOUS.

SECT. II. CARTILAGINOUS.

VI. RAY

VI. RAY	Thorn-back	C. *App.*	
	Sting	C. *App.*	
	Devil-fish	C. *App.*	
VII. SHARK	White ?	C. *App.*	
	Saw	Squalus Priflis. C. *App.*	
VIII. FISHING FROG	Common	Br. *Zool.* C. *App.*	
IX. STURGEON	European	*ib.*	
	Blunt-nofed	*Muf. Bl.*	
X. BALISTES	Unicorn	B. monoceros.	C. II. 19
	Hifpid	B. hifpidus	
	Old	B. vetula.	C. II. 22
XI. TETRODON	Smooth	T. lævigatus	
	Globe	T. lagocephalus	C. II. 28
	Sun	Br. *Zool.* C. *App.*	
XII. LUMP	Lump-fish	Br. *Zcol.*	
XIII. PIPE-FISH	Shorter	*ib.*	

SECT. III. BONY.

* APODAL.

XIV. EEL	Muray	Muræna Helena. C. II. 20. 21	
	Eel	Br. *Zool.*	
	Conger	*ib.*	
XV. SWORD	Sword-fish	*ib.*	

XVI. COD		* * JUGULAR	
	Common	*ib.*	
	Froft	Gadus callarias. *Muf. Bl.*	
	Tau	Gadus Tau.	
XVII. BLENNY	puftulated	N. S. *Mr. B.*	

XVIII. REMORA		* * * THORACIC.	
	Remora	Ech. neucrates.	C. II. 26
XIX. CORYPHÆNE	Parrot	C. Pfittacus	C. II. 29
	Blue	C. II. 18	
	Lineated	C. lineata	

XX. BULL-

XX. Bull-head	Father-lasher	Br. Zool.

XXI. Flounder	Holibut	Br. Zool.
	Flounder	ib.
	Plaise	ib.
	Rough	Pleuronectes plagiusa
	Sole	Br. Zool.
	Lineated	Pl. lineatus
	Lunated	Pl. lunata C. II. 27

XXII. Chætodon	Scalelefs	Ch. alepidotus
	Angel	Ch. triostegus C. II. 31

XXIII. Gilthead	Lane fnapper	Sparus fynagris C. II. 17
	Pork-fish	Sp. rhomboides C. II. 4
	Porgy	Sp. chryfops C. II. 16
	Silver	Sp. argyrops.
	Radiated	Sp. radiatus. C. II. 12
	Virginian	Sp. virginicus

XXIV. Wrasse	Mutton	Labrus anthias C. II. 25
	Mangrove	L. grifeus C. II. 9
	Hog	L. flavus C. II. 11
	Gaper	L. hiatula
	Drum	L. chromis C. App. XXXIII.
	Yellow	L. fulvus C. II. 10
	Cinereous	C. II. 11. fig. 2
	Bone	C. II. 13
	Great ?	C. II. 15

XXV. Perch	River ?	Br. Zool. C. App.
	Yellow-bellied	Labrus auritus. C. II. 8
	Dotted	Perca punctata
	Whiting ?	P. albarnus. C. II. 12
	Croker	P. undulata C. II. 3.
	Eyed	P. ocellata
	Noble	P. nobilis
	Philadelphian	P. Philadelphica
	Black	P. atraria
	Margate	P. chryfopiera C. II. 2
	Negro	P. punctata C. II. 7
	Hind	P. guttata C. II. 14
	Venemous	P. venenofa C. II. 5
	Black-tail	P. melanura C. II. 7

Rudder

	Rudder	P. fectatrix C. II. 8
	Striated	P. ftriata
	Grunt	P. formofa C. II. 6
	Trifurcated	P. trifurca
	Bafs ?	*Br. Zool. C. App.* XXXIII.
	Apodal	C. II. 4.
XXVI. STICKLE-BACK	Crevalle	Gafterofteus Carolinus
	Canada	G. Canadus
	Skip-Jack	G. Saltatrix. C. II. 14
	Two-fpined	*Muf. Bl.*
XXVII. MACKREL	Yellow-tail	Scomber Hippos
XXVIII. GURNARD	Flying	Trigla evolans
	Rough	N. S. *Muf. Bl.*

* * * *

ABDOMINAL.

XXIX. LOCH	Beardlefs	Cobitis heteroclita
XXX. AMIA	Mud-fifh	Amia calva
XXXI. SILURE	Cat	Silurus felis. S. catus. C. II. 23
	Armed	S. cataphractus. C. III. 19
XXXII. TROUT	Salmon	*Br. Zool.*
	Trout	*Br. Zool. Mr. B.*
	White fifh	Salmo lavarettus ?
	Long	S. fœtens. C. II. 2
XXXIII. PIKE	Fox	Efox vulpes. C. II. 1
	Green	E. Offeus. C. II. 30
	Sea-needle	*Br. Zool*
	Under-jaw	E. Brafilienfis. *Mr. B.*
	Barracuda	C. II. 1
	Common	*Br. Zool. C. App.*
XXXIV. ELOPS	Forked	El. Saurus
XXXV. ARGENTINE	Caroline	Arg. Carolina. C. II. 24 *

* Perhaps a herring.

XXXVI.

XXXVI. ATHERINE	Silver-fish	Ath. menidia
XXXVII. MULLET	White	Mugil albula. C. II. 6
	Common	*Br. Zool.* *C. App.*
XXXVIII. POLYNEME	Virginian	P. Virginicus
XXXIX. HERRING	Common	*Br. Zool.*
	Shad	*ib. C. App.* XXXII
XL. CARP.	Common	*Br. Zool. C. App.*
	Roach	*ib.* *ib.*
	Dace	*ib.* *ib.*
	Mummy-Chog.	N. S. *Muf. Bl.*

————————

CLASS V. INSECTS.

SECT. I. BEETLES.

*

I. CHAFER Scarabæus lunaris. *Muf. Bl.*
aloëus
lancifer
naficornis
Carolinus
mimas
carnifex
nuchicornis
Marianus
ftercorarius
Amazonus
Surinamus
nitidus
fepicola
horticola, a variety
occidentalis
lanigerus
fafciatus
Indus
brunnus
punctatus

nobilis

nobilis
quadrimaculatus
Hudfonias. *Drury* t. 35. f. 7 N.
  S. *Muf. Bl.*
rufus. N. S.   *Muf. Bl.*
lævipes. N. S.   *Muf. Bl.*
piceus. N. S.   *Muf. Bl.*
biunguiculatus, N. S.   *Muf. Bl.*
pilofus. N. S.   *Muf. Bl.*
teftaceus. N. S.   *Muf. Bl.*

II. STAG-BEETLE	Lucanus	cervus

capreolus
interruptus
— — — *N. B.* a brown variety

III, LEATHER-EATER	Dermeftes	lardarius

capucinus
typographus
fafciatus. N. S.   *Muf. Bl,*

IV. MIMICK-BEETLE	Hifter	unicolor

V. WHIRL-BEETLE	Gyrinus	Americanus

VI. CARRION-BEETLE	Silpha	vefpillo. *N. B.* a great variety, and

the fmall one too
noveboracenfis. N. S.   *Muf. Bl,*
bipuftulata
quadripuftulata
Americana
obfcura
aquatica

VII. WEEVIL	Curculio	noveboracenfis. N. S. *Muf. Bl,*

palmarum
Bacchus
difpar
anchoraco
nucum
incanus
fcutellatus. N. S.   *Muf. Bl.*

VIII. NUT-BEETLE	Attelabus	curculionoides

Penfylvanicus.

IX. LADY-

IX. LADY-FLY	Coccinella	impunctata
		7-punctata
		13-punctata
		2-pustulata

❋ ❋

X. GLOW-WORM	Lampyris	Pyralis
		marginata
		pilofa. N. S. *Muf. Bl.*

| XI. SEED-BEETLE | Bruchus Pifi | *Kalm* I. 173—177 |

XII. GOLDEN-HONEY-	Chryfomela	5-punctata
BEETLE		occidentalis
		Boleti
		Philadelphica
		3-maculata
		Americana
		lineola
		bicolor, variety with red thighs, *Muf. Bl.*
		fcopolina
		obfcura
		10-maculata
		12-punctata
		Phellandrii
		tomentofa
		Rhoi. N. S. *Muf. Bl.*
		fpinicornis. N. S. *Muf. Bl.*
		lepturoides. N. S. *Muf. Bl.*
		lineato-punctata. N.S. *Muf. Bl.*
		trifurcata. N. S. *Muf. Bl.*
		laticlavia. N. S. *Muf. Bl.*
		fimbriata. N. S. *Muf. Bl.*
		frontalis. N. S. *Muf. Bl.*
		Hudfonias. N. S. *Muf. Bl.*

XIII. BLISTER-BEETLE	Meloë	veficatorius
		majalis
		cinerea. N. S. *Muf. Bl.*

| XIV. STINKING-BEETLE | Tenebrio | chalybeus |
| | | Mauritanicus |

culinaris

culinaris
foffor

XV. Tortoise-beetle Caffida   viridis
bipuftula ? *Muf. Bl.*

* * *

XVI. Glossy-beetle Cicindela   hybrida
Germanica
riparia

XVII. Ground-beetle Carabus   granulatus, **γ.**
hortenfis
leucophthalmus
inquifitor
lividus, fmall variety
marginatus
crepitans
Americanus
cyanocephalus
vulgaris
piceus
fericeus. N. S. *Muf. Bl.*
fafciatus. N. S. *Muf. Bl.*

XVIII. Burn-cow Bupreftis   gigantea
mariana
chryfoftigma
Auftriaca

XIX. Spring-beetle Elater   oculatus
phofporeus
ligneus ?
obfcurus

XX. Water-beetle Dytifcus   fufcipes
marginatus

XXI. Softwinged-Beetle Malacopteryx Americauus. N. S. *Muf. Bl.*
Cantharis   tropica

XXII. Wood-beetle Leptura   myftica
detrita
       Robiniæ.

		Robiniæ. *Drury.* t. 41. f. 2.
		N. S. *Muf. Bl.*
		Americana. N. S. *Muf. Bl.*
		nitens
XXIII. CAPRICORN-BEETLE.	Cerambyx	imbricornis
		coriarius, variety
		melanopus
		lineatus
		fpinibarbis
		araneiformis
		4-maculatus
		fuccinctus
		fuaveolens
		Coquus
		hifpicornis. *Drury.* t. 41. f. 4.
		rufticus
		bajulus
		tetrophthalmus. N. S. *Muf. Bl.*
		brunnus. N. S. *Muf. Bl.*
		palliatus. N. S. *Muf. Bl.*
		clavipes. N. S. *Muf. Bl.*

* * * *

XXIV. ROVE-BEETLE	Staphylinus	hirtus
		erythropterus

XXV. CLIPT-WINGED BEETLE	Necydalis	collaris. N. S. *Muf. Bl.*

XXVI. EARWIG	Forficula	auricularia

SECT. II. HALFWINGED INSECTS.

XXVII. COCKROACH	Blatta	Americana
		Orientalis
		Germanica
		livida. N. S. *Muf. Bl.*

XXVIII. CAMELCRICKET	Mantis	irrorata
		Carolina

XXIX. LOCUST	Gryllus	brevicornis
		gryllotalpa
		campeftris

citrifolius

		citrifolius
		laurifolius
		myrtifolius ?
		fuccinctus
	◆	criftatus
		Carolinus

XXX. FLEA-LOCUST	Cicada	fquamigera
		tibicen
	◆	feptendecim
		violacea
		fpumaria
		phalænoides
		Lanio
		carinata. N. S. *Muf. Bl.*
		guttata. N. S. *Muf. Bl.*
		coccinea. N. S. *Muf. Bl.*

| XXXI. BOAT-FLY | Notonecta | glauca |
| | | lineata. N. S. *Muf. Bl.* |

| XXXII. WATERSCORPION | Nepa | grandis |

XXXIII. BUG	Cimex	lecticularis. *Kalm.*
		bidens
		ictericus
		floridanus
		hæmorrhous
		baccarum
		prafinus
		biguttatos, variety with red dots
		and marges
		criftatus
		trifafciatus
		fuccinctus
		lacuftris

| XXXIV. PLANTSUCKER | Chermes | Alni. *Kalm* |

| XXXV. COCHINEAL | Coccus | Cacti. *Bartram's Florida* |

SECT. III.

SECT. III. PAPILIONACEOUS. INSECTS.

XXXVI. BUTTERFLY	Papilio	Troilus. *Drury.* t. 11. f. 1—5 ?
		Ajax. *Edw.* 34.
		Xuthus. *Drury.* t. 22. f. 1. 2.
		Antilochus
		Podalirius
		Protefilaus. *Drury.* t. 22. f. 34.
		Apollo. *Muf. Bl.*
		Braſſicæ
		Hyale
		Eubule
		Ecclipſis
		Midamus
		Plexippus
		Miſippus
		Chryſippus
		Canthus
		Almana
		Orithya
		Cardui
		Antiopa. *Kalm.*
		urticæ
		C. album.
		Atalanta
		Euphroſyne. *Kalm.*
		Cupido
		quercus
		Echion
		Virgaureæ
		Bixæ
XXXVII. HAWK-MOTH	Sphinx	ocellata
		Populi
		Carolina
		Celerio
		Pinaſtri
		fuciformis. β. Tityus
XXXVII. MOTH	Phalæna	Atlas
		Cecropia
		Paphia

Luna

Luna
Virgo
Plantaginis
Chryforrhœa
lubricipeda
paranympha
Gamma
Pfi
bilineata
viridana
bella
pulchella

S E C T. IV. INSECTS with nervous Wings.

XXXIX. DRAGON-FLY	Libellula	flaveola
		depreffa
		ænea
		umbrata
		Americana
		Carolina
XL. CAMEL-FLY	Raphidia	cornuta
XLI. SPRING-FLY	Phryganea	bicaudata
XLII. PEARL-FLY	Hemerobius	pectinicornis
XLIII. SCORPION-FLY	Panorpa	communis

S E C T. V. INSECTS with Stings.

XLIV. BEE	Apis	cordata
		mellifica
		roftrata
		violacea
		Carolina
		pratorum
		æftuans
		noveboracenfis N. S. *Muf. Bl.*
		vefpiformis. N. S. *Muf. Bl.*
		fericea. N. S. *Muf. Bl.*

XLV.

XLV. Ant	Formica	herculeana rufa
XLVI. Wasp	Vefpa	Carolina maculata. *Muf. Bl* annularis quadridens Canadenfis
XLVII. Golden Wall-fly		Chryfis cyanea
XLVIII. Tailed Wasp	Sirex	Columba. *Muf. Bl.*
XLIX. Saw-fly	Tenthredo	fcrophulariæ lutea viridis
L. Ichneumon Wasp	Sphex	fabulofa cœrulea Penfylvanica arenaria
LI. Ichneumon-fly	Ichneumon	luteus
LII. Naked Bee	Mutilla	occidentalis

S E C T. VI.   Two-winged Insects.

LIII. Gnat	Culex	pipiens. *Mufquito* pulicaris
LIV. Wasp-fly	Afilus	æftuans gibbofus
LV. Flower-breeze	Bombylius	minor. *Muf. Bl.*
LVI. Horse-fly	Hippobofca	hirundinis. *Muf. Bl.*

LVII.

LVII. FLY	Mufca	illucens. Drury, t. 44. f. 1. *M. Bl.*
		leucopa
		vomitoria
		carnaria
		domeftica
LVIII. WHAME	Tabanus	Americanus. N. S. *Muf. Bl.*
LIX. GADFLY	Oeftrus	Tarandi

S E C T. VII. INSECTS without Wings

LX. SUGARMITE	Lepifma	faccharina
LXI. GROUND-FLEA	Podura	aquatica
LXII. DEATH-WATCH	Termes	pulfatorium
LXIII. LOUSE	Pediculus	humanus
		ricinoides
		fuis
		cervi
		meleagridis
LXIV. FLEA	Pulex	irritans
		penetrans. *Chigger*
LXV. TICK	Acarus	Americanus
		Siro
		holofericeus
LXVI. LONG-LEGGED SPIDER	Phalangium	groffipes
		opilio
		acaroides
		balænarum
		reniforme
LXVII. SPIDER	Aranea	diadema
		clavipes
		venatoria
LXVIII. SCOR-PION	Scorpio	Americanus
		auftralis. *Muf. Bl.*

LXIX.

LXIX. CRABFISH.   fentry   Cancer pinnophylax
                  minute   C. minutus. *Kalm.*
                  land   C. ruricola. *Cat.* II. 32.
                  florid   C. floridus
                  Sand   C. vocans. *Cat.* II. 35.
                  common   C. mænas. *Mr. B.*
                  roughfhelled C. granulatus. *Cat.* II. 36. N° 2.
                  fpider   C. araneus. *Mr. B.*
                  dòtted   C. punctatûs
                  rock   C. Grapfus. *Cat.* II. 36. N° 1.
                  redclawed *Cat.* II. 37. f 1.

LXX. LOBSTER   common   Cancer Gammarus
                  cynic   C. Diogenes. *Cat.* II. 33. f. 1. 2.
                  Soldier   *Cat.* II. 34
                  Cray   C. carcinus

LXXI. MONOCULE   King's Crab Monoculus Polyphemus. *Muf. Bl.*

LXXII. MILLEPEE   Onifcus   Oeftrum. *Muf. Bl.*
                              Phyfodes. *Muf. Bl.*
                              Ceti
                              Afellus

LXXIII. CENTIPEE Scolopendra forficata
                              morfitans. *Cat.* II. 2.
                              occidentalis
                              marina

LXXIV. GALLYWORM Julus   craffus

T E S T A C E O U S.

REFERENCES to American Shells, engraved in Lifter's Hift. Conch.

LAND	Nº 19	Sea Bivalves. Nº 34. 279
	45	196. 358
	69	200. 434
	82	277. 436
	91	Sea turbinated. 855. a. 12
	92	1058.—10
	93	1059—2
	94	4

RIVER TURBINATED	3	River Bivalve	5
	4		6
	5		9
	6		10
	7		15
	8		
	35		
	44		
	45		
	46		

SHORT

SHORT DIRECTIONS

For LOVERS and PROMOTERS of

NATURAL HISTORY,

In what manner Specimens of all Kinds may be collected, preserved, and transported to distant Countries.

I. ALL Quadrupeds of a great bulk must be skinned as soon as possible after death; the tail, claws, teeth, horns, ears, bristles on the nose and chin, are carefully to be preserved; the hair of the fur as little stained with blood as possible; the opening is to be as small as it can conveniently be without hindering the operation; the inside of the skin may then be washed or brushed over with a liquor, made of an ounce of Sal Ammoniac, dissolved in a quart of water, in which afterwards two ounces of corrosive sublimate Mercury must be put: or four ounces of Arsenic may be boiled in two quarts, or two quarts and a half of water, till all or the greater part of it be dissolved, and the liquor may serve for the same purpose to wash the inside of the skin: then the whole cavity must be stuffed with oakum or tow, likewise saturated with the above liquor, afterwards dried and mixed

with

with a powder of four parts of Tobacco-fand, four parts
of pounded black Pepper, one part of burnt Alum, and
one part of corrofive Sublimate or Arfenic : laftly, the
whole is to be fewed with a thread dipt in the above liquor,
and the fkin thus ftuffed muft be gently dried, and a day
after put into an oven, whofe heat muft be fo gentle, that
a hair, or a feather put for trial's fake into it, will not
crifp, or curl, or bend; and thus it will be perfectly
dried : the eyes may be filled up with putty, which, when
dry, will look like the white part of an eye, and will bear
painting, to exprefs with oil-colours the iris and pupil of
the natural eye of the animal in queftion. The whole
animal muft be put into a box, filled with tow or mofs, or
oakum fteeped in the above liquor, and perfectly dried.
The box muft be brufhed over on both fides with the above
liquor, and dried; and the crevices fhut up with pieces of
paper pafted over; the pafte muft be made either with the
arfenical liquor, or that made with corrofive fublimate
inftead of common water; and I can affure thefe precau-
tions, though cheap and fimple, will keep the animal in
the beft prefervation on the longeft voyages, and for many
years in a collection. This way of preparing and fecuring
the boxes for fending fpecimens abroad, the prepared
oakum or tow, the powder and liquor mentioned above,
are always to be underftood when I afterwards fpeak of
prepared boxes, prepared tow, mofs, or oakum, and preparing powder or liquor.

II. Small Quadrupeds may be plunged into a keg of
brandy, rack or rum, and thus fent over : obferve however to put them firft into the coarfer kind of fpirits;
and after they have been therein for a while, and parted
with fome impurities, you muft put them into another
veffel with new clean rum or brandy, into which fome
alum may be put; and they will keep thus better, and
be lefs fubject to change or decay.

III. Birds muft be opened at the vent, their entrails,
lungs,

lungs, and craws taken out, wafhed with the above preparing liquor, ftrewed with the preparing powder, ftuffed with the prepared oakum or tow; their plumage kept clean during the operation, fewed up with thread fteeped in the preparing liquor; the eyes taken out, with the tongue, and both places wafhed with the fame liquor; the mouth muft be filled with prepared tow in great birds; the eyes filled up with putty, and, when dry, painted with oil-colour after the natural colour of live birds of the fame fpecies, and then dried in an oven: however, as there is all the meat on the bird left, care muft be taken not to take too plump or too fat birds, and dry them flowly under the fame precaution as mentioned N° I. The operation muft be repeated till the bird be perfectly dry. The attitude may be given to the bird before he be put into the oven, by wires that are fharp on one end, and thrufted through the bird's legs, body, breaft, and neck, and others going through the wings and body. Small birds are likewife well preferved in brandy, rack, or rum; and when arrived at the place of their deftination, they muft be wafhed and fweetened in frefh water for feveral times, and laftly dipped in the preparing liquor, the plumage laid in order, the attitude given to the bird by wires, and then dried. Care muft be taken to kill the birds with fhot proportioned to their fize, and at a reafonable diftance, that the fpecimen may not be mangled and torn. Young birds which have not yet moulted, muft not be taken, but old birds in full feather, and, if poffible, a fpecimen of each fex; for the fexes often vary very much in fize, feather, and colour. The nefts of birds and their eggs would likewife contribute towards perfecting the hiftory of this branch of zoology.

IV. All kinds of Reptiles, as fnakes, lizards, and frogs, and fmall tortoifes, muft be put into brandy or rum with alum in it: obferve not to take fuch fnakes or lizards as have accidentally loft their tails: the fcales of thefe animals muft be carefully preferved.

V. Fifh

V. Fith of all denominations will likewife bear fending in bottles or kegs with brandy or rum. The fins, and tails of the fith, their fcales, and in fome kinds, the beards, or other fmall characteriftic appendages, muft not be rubbed, torn, or deftroyed.

VI. Infects may be caught in a pair of forceps covered with fine green or white gauze, which for better fecurity may be fewed over either with filk or thread. The collec-tor muft have a pincufhion, with three or four different fizes of pins, calculated for the different fizes of the in-fects; one or two chip-boxes lined on top and bottom with cork, all fteeped in the preparing liquor; one or more larger ftore-boxes at home to put therein the infects caught in the various excurfions; a large Mufcheto gauze-net made in the fhape of a bat fowling-net, which is to be got ready made in London; and a thread net with fmall mefhes on a round wire hoop fixed to a long pole, in order thus to catch infects that live in water. With thefe inftruments all infects may eafily be caught. The beetles muft have the pin run through one of their wing-fhells; the half-winged infects through the thorax, and fo likewife muft be done to butterflies, hawk-moths, and moths, to the in-fects with four and two membranaceous wings, and fome of the infects without wings. As the papilionaceous infects very frequently beat their wings, and thus rub off the fine fcales covering them, it is neceffary to give thefe creatures, when in the forceps or net, a gentle fqueeze at the infertion of the wings in the body, and to put them, when returned home from an excurfion, on a large pincufhion, by which means they will be enabled to reft their feet on, and this will prevent their fluttering. Beetles, and many of the half-winged infects, may be dipped in the preparing liquor, which will kill and put them foon out of pain and pre-vent fmall infects from deftroying them. The greater part of beetles may with as great propriety be plunged into a

bottle,

bottle, with rum or rack, and thus fent over. This can likewife be done with all marine infects, fmall crabs, millepees, centipees, fpiders, gally worms, fcorpions, &c. and many curious grubs or caterpillars, which are the firft ftate which beetles and butterflies, moths, &c. live in. To each infect, not in fpirits, put a fmall paper, on which is marked the time of the year it is caught in, the plant or food it lives upon, its changes, and what animals feaft again upon the infect, and other fuch particularities.

VII. The fhells, both thofe found in frefh water-lakes, ponds, and rivers, and thofe that live only in the ocean, muft not be chofen among thofe that lie on the fhores of the fea and frefh waters, and have been broken and injured, or rolled by the waves and expofed to the air and fun and thus calcined ; but rather as frefh as poffible, and with the animal in it : one or two fpecimens of which may be preferved in Spirits : from the reft extract the animal, and keep the fhell, when perfectly dry and fweet, packed up in cotton, tow, or mofs. The fame is to be done with the echini or fea-eggs, and other cruftaceous animals ; efpecially be careful to preferve their curious fpines.

VIII. The harder and ftone-like animal productions of the fea, comprehended under the names of Madrepores, Millepores, Cellepores, Corals, and Gorgonias, are either without its inhabitants, and then they want no other care but a good packing in cotton or tow ; or the animal is ftill alive, and then it would be neceffary to put the fpecimen in a flat veffel filled with Sea-water, and to watch the moment when the animal puts out its arms or branches, and then to pour inftantly a good quantity of ftrong fpirit into the water, fo that the acid of the liquor may prevent the animal from drawing in its branches or arms : after this, the animal may be

put

put into another glafs, with new rum poured on it; the glafs muft be well corked, and covered with putty and a bladder. All the alcyoniums, fpunges, hornwracks, pipe-corals, coralines, fea-feathers, and other curious zoophytes, muft be treated in the fame manner; as this would be a means to acquaint us with the various inhabitants of this curious tribe of marine productions.

IX. The various worm-like animals comprehended under the name of *Mollufca*, may be beft preferved in rum or brandy: only obferve to pour the rum on them, when they are putting out their arms, eyes, horns, tentacula, and other parts of their frame.

X. To the quadrupeds, birds, reptiles, fifh, and in general to all the fpecimens, muft be fixed lead tickets by means of a wire, and a number on the lead fcratched in; which muft be referred to, in a paper, where under the fame number the collector would be pleafed to write the name by which the animal goes in his country, or among the various tribes of Indian nations, with the food, age, growth, nature, manners, haunts, how many young or eggs it brings forth, in what manner it is caught, what it is ufed for, &c. &c.

XI. The vegetable world affords fuch an immenfe variety of productions of fo great and varied ufes for the various purpofes and wants of human fociety; that it would be rather blameable in men to be indolent in refpect to them. Old England can juftly glory in being poffeffed of the greateft variety of plants of all kinds; but even thefe glorious and fpirited efforts in this branch of knowledge, are not yet fufficient to make us acquainted with all the productions of the vegetable kingdom, and their various ufes. Befides this, their cultivation at large is often impoffible in our cold climate, and referved for a more mild and happy one,

beyond

beyond the Atlantic: nothing is therefore more nè-
ceffary than to facilitate the tranfportation of feeds and
plants into diftant countries in a ftate of vegetation.
The ingenious and great promoter of natural hiftory,
John Ellis, Efq; has favoured the world with a curious
pamphlet, containing the beft directions for that purpofe;
it would be therefore fuperfluous to repeat what he has
already faid, were it not neceffary to make my perform-
ance more compleat, by inferting a few hints abftracted
from his ufeful publication; and adding to it fome re-
marks of my own.

Seeds of all kinds, intended to be fent abroad, muft
be collected perfectly ripe in dry weather, and kept dry
without expofing them to funfhine. Hard nuts, and
leguminous feeds, may be plunged for a moment in the
preparing liquor and then dried again, as this would
prevent infects from attacking them. In general muft
the feeds be previoufly examined, and care taken that
no infects may be fent with them; this can fometimes
be difcovered by the naked eye, fometimes by a magnify-
ing glafs, and by a little brown or black fpot on the out-
fide of the feed; fuch ripe and chofen feeds, if of a good
fize, each of them may be wrapped in a flat piece of
bees-wax; if fmall or quite minute, many may be put
together in fuch a piece of bees-wax, or, what is ftill
better, in a piece of cerate paper, i. e. paper fteeped in
melted bees-wax, and all thefe parcels muft be put in a
pot or box, proportionate to the quantity of feeds you
have, filled with melted wax, to the height of about the
fize of the feeds you are to fend, or the parcels you have
made; and when the wax is pretty cool, but ftill foft,
lay your feeds or parcels in rows in the foft wax, and then
fill again fome melted wax in, and proceed to lay feeds
in the fame manner till your pot or box be full. Pulpy
feeds, as thofe of ftrawberries, mulberries, arbutus's,

may

may be fqueezed together, preffing out the watery par-
ticles, drying thefe fmall cakes, and then putting them
in the abovementioned cerate paper. Or fmall feeds mixed
with dry fand, and put in cerate paper, packed in proportionate glaffes, and covered with a bladder or leather,
and all fuch glaffes again packed in a veffel, filled with a
mixture, confifting of half culinary falt, the other half
of two parts of faltpetre, and one part of fal ammoniac,
will keep the feeds cool, and preferve their vegetative
power.

Plants or fhrubs that are to be tranfported, muft
be taken out with a lump of foil covering the roots,
which muft be wrapped in wet mofs, furrounded with
paper or a Ruffian baft-mat and packthread ; plants
thus packed may be put in a cheft or box upon a
layer of three inches deep wet mofs in clofe rows, fill-
ing up all vacancies with mofs. Some holes or flips in
the lid of the box, covered with baft-mats or fail-cloth,
will give them air, and a direction muft be fixed on
top, to keep the lid uppermoft, and the box in an open
but fhady airy place, out of the fpray of the fea : the
fame caution, in regard to air and fea, muft be taken
with the boxes containing feeds.

XII. Minerals, foffils, and petrefactions of all kinds,
ought to be wrapt feparately in papers, and the whole
collection packed in hay, tow, hemp, or cotton, in a box,
fo that none of the fpecimens may touch or rub one
another when the box is tranfported by land-carriage,
or fhaken by the rolling of the fea. Clays, earths,
fands, and falts, are beft preferved in glaffes, or little
glazed gally-pots covered with a bladder. Mineral waters may be fafely filled in glafs bottles, immediately after corked up and pitched, or covered with putty round
the cork.

XIII.

XIII. Though antiquities are no ways in connection with Natural History, it will however, be very acceptable, if the curious of North America will collect and communicate to their friends in Great Britain, all the inscriptions, arms, vases, utensils, idols, and other things, found in that continent, capable of throwing a light on the history and antiquities of its first inhabitants.

In the Catalogue of North American animals are some omitted, and some discovered since the publication that pamphlet, and I therefore found it most convenient to put them here by way of supplement.

Page 6. Sect. 11. before II. Sheep put			Penn. Syn.
Ox. American.	*Eur.*	Quad. No.	6,
8. Genus II. Falcon before Bald Eagle,			
Golden Eagle. F. chrysaëtos.	Bossu I. p. 288.		
10. Genus XIII. Creeper, add		C. I.	61.
after common,			
Pine Certhia pinus.			
Ibid. Before Genus XV. Turkey			
BUSTARD, common, otis tarda	Bossu I. p. 94.		
18. Among the Snakes,			
Eggeater. Coluber ovivorus			
22. Before Genus XXXII.			
Trout, Insert			
LEATHERFISH Tang Teuthis hepatus.		C. II.	10.
Ibid. Before Genus XXXIII. PIKE. Add			
WHIPTAIL forked Fistularia tabaccaria		C. II.	17,
23. Before Genus XXXVIII. Polyneme.			
FLYING FISH. Common Exocoetus volitans.	*Kalm.*		
Round evolans.		C. II.	8,
Ibid. At the bottom of the page Scarabæus Lanius	*Drury*	t. 33. f. 8.	
			Page

Page 27. Among the Cerambyces.
    Cerambyx irroratus   *Drury*   t. 41. f. 3.
Ibid. Genus XXVIII. CAMEL-
    CRICKET Mantis, add,
      Mantis Gongylodes.   *Drury*   t. 50. f. 2.
  28. Before Genus XXX.
    Gryllus tataricus   *Drury.*   t. 49. f. 2.
  30. Under Genus XXXIX. Dra-
    gon-fly.
    Libellula Virgo γ   *Drury*   t. 48. f. 2.
Ibid. After Genus XLIII. put
ANT-LION, Myrmeleon Formicalyn.   *Drury*   t. 46. f. 4.